Wasteland Daydreams

Alyssa Lister

BookLeaf Publishing

India | USA | UK

Presentation by *BookLeaf Publishing*

Web: www.bookleafpub.com

E-mail: info@bookleafpub.com

ISBN: 9789358319934

First edition 2023

DEDICATION

To the man who will never know me. You have been my muse for many years.

ACKNOWLEDGEMENT

I would like to thank BookLeaf Publishing for this opportunity to get my works out there even if it's just a one time thing. I wanna thank future readers who decide to pick up this book and who will give me constructive criticism so I can make other works better in the future. I also wanna thank my sister, my mother, and my friend Kat for their support in my crazy creative endeavors.

PREFACE

These poems are for me to work out the complex world we live in as I try to describe what each moment means to me. I'm having to come face to face with things I don't know. I can't tell what's real and what's not in an age where everything is digitalized. It's exhausting and all I want to do is go back to daydreaming of romance I'll never have and dreams I may never bring to reality. I'll end up wasting my life away if I'm not careful.

The man yet to reawaken

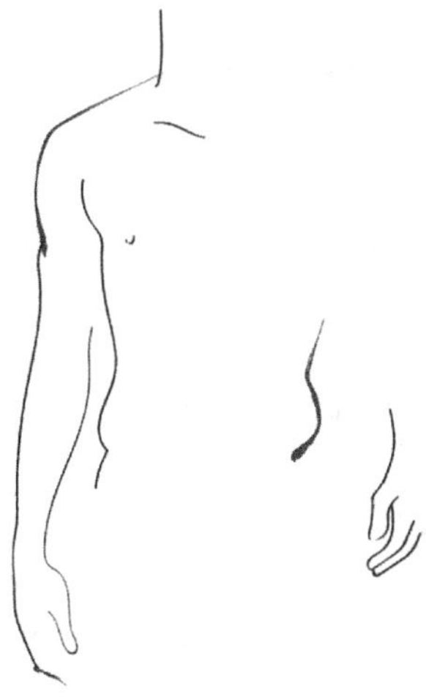

He was a marble sculpture

Timeless and well-defined

Every curl that mapped his head,

every muscle, every veiny detail

was carefully pondered over by its creator

His stoic face remained unbothered

by the heavy burden upon his shoulders

I can still picture the emeralds of his eyes,

stormy and restless beneath those long lashes

If I kissed his thin lips now, would it bring him
back to life?

Could beauty wake the sleeping beast?

Would he still be troubled by the past?

Or remain oblivious to those memories we
shared?

Of when his thumb brushed over my soft lips
before

Leaning down, his hands in my hair, bruising
my lips with his own

As he indulged me with the seeds of a
pomegranate

I know what it meant as he did this and what it
meant when I accepted his offer

Whenever I was at his side, I was glowing

A beauty that I never knew before him

Never was my smile so honest

My eyes never sparkled so bright

I have never danced with such grace 'til I began
this waltz with him

I plead for him to reawaken

I plead for death not to take him just yet

I plead with God for another chance

Worst of me

I am frail

I am selfish

I am gluttonous

I am lustful

I am murderous

I am unkind

The darkest of thoughts remain in the back of
my mind

I wish I could say that who you see is what I am
but

There's a devil underneath

A broken vessel

Push the right buttons and I could be no better
than a killer or a thief
I will make you angry. I will give you grief. I
will give you no peace.

You will feel contempt

You will be heartbroken

You will leave

So that I will remain lonely

Where I am safe; I am secure

I am comforted by the void

As the door behind you closes

For the final time,

In the pits of regret,

I wish you were still by my side

I love alone

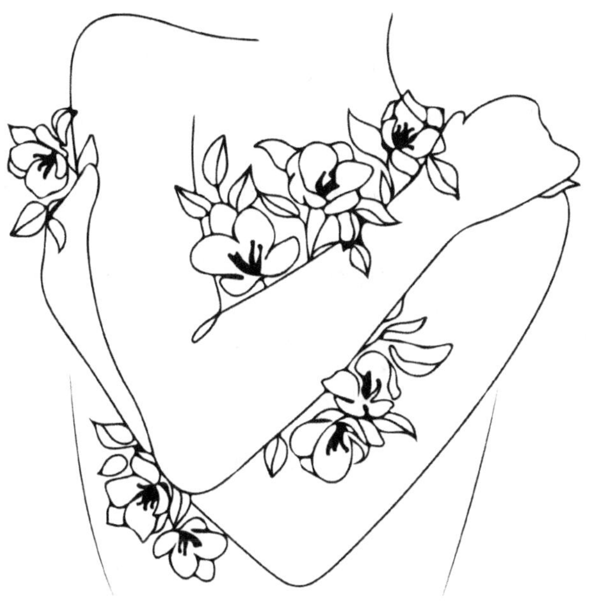

I love too much, a little too quick

Point to my theatrics and dramatic exit

I love I love I love

A man I'm enraptured by has humility and a
well-rounded masculine tendency

Loyalty to him is unwavering despite the other
pretty men around me

But the men in my thoughts are not always who
I thought them to be

Will we ever know if the one we have chosen is
the right one?

Can I take the risk? The leap of faith?

Susceptible to change we are, good or bad.

Societal pressures, and stresses of life, can they
contend with it?

Will they allow the demon's seductive whispers
to distort their perceptions?

Can they put in the work to grow and bloom into
something new?

Broken heart be damned I'd say. I'm not afraid
of feeling sorrow.

Embrace my woes, hold their hand 'til I'm better
again.

Pick myself up and try again.

Solitary life is overhyped and lonely too.

I'll wait, wait, and wait if I have to. I have no
need to rush.

It's something to process, contemplate and
cherish.

I will not be in contempt I say!

I'll love even if it seems that I love alone.

Women cannot be redefined

Women cannot be redefined

We set society on its course

For we teach right from wrong in our children
and

know exactly when to quiet the monster into a
light slumber in the men

who run it in our stead

The protection we are given and the gentle
kindness we give

Is nothing compared to the subtle power we hold

Good men are beholden to our expectations

as they yearn for the soft caresses of a good
woman upon them

You will never know what it will be like to be
cared for under the wings of a

humble gentleman in the same way we feel

You will never know the fear of every risk we
take due to innate vulnerabilities

we cherish

You will never share the same emotions, societal
fears, and inner demons in the

the same way we do.

We women are in sync with each other like the
moon to the ocean waves.

Our thoughts, our wants, our needs, and
everything we do are for a similar goal,

we just pursue it in different ways.

We compete, we hurt, we rip each other apart.

we are brutal yet we are subtle, we torture each
other. We go after enemies'

reputations 'til their lives are in tatters

For the sake of a diamond on our finger and our
children have a father
It's just the way evolution has programmed us
for the sake of our genetics.

Evolution is not to be underestimated.

So don't ever say we are one of the same.

My womaness is not for you to take and twist
into your abhorrent desires.

My innate identity is not a kink or a dress to put
on.

You should be ashamed to think otherwise.

Deep Black

The clock tick-tocks, the labyrinth never ends

Uncertainty and a dreadful heaviness blur my
perception

Whispers of things I want to hear, voices
starving for my attention with deceitful truths
and rancorous compassion

Half-truths burden me and make me hopeless as
I will never be enlightened

Every decision, every door to take remains
unclear

As the screeching and growling grow closer and
closer,

Heavy feet stomping grows louder and louder

I jump into the void to hide from my angels and
my demons

The chattering ceased as silence embraced me,

I gave up my world, my values, my beliefs,
my warring mind to curl up in a ball in the deep
black,

I am comforted in the nothingness as I am
content to remain hidden for all

eternity.

To be in love

Come love me 'til my heart breaks

I don't mind, I wanna sink into you

So deserving of me

I am in awe of who you are

I am yours forevermore

I will await death for you

As I am not ashamed that I love you

I can't fathom being but

I see the good in you

Come to me when you are ready for paradise

Remember heaven when you close your eyes

Shake off the heavy shackles that keep you on
your knees
Stand up with your head held high

Accept my hand as we wander deep into hell

Purify the black sun in your veins

Make a new reality for what you dream

Build a home for me in your heart

To Be In Love

My teardrops are like red wine

Drink up the ambrosia

The Lacrima

Maybe just this once you'll see what I see

You got my mind and body

You have full control for just this moment

To be In Love

Tear my heart open

In the cavern, it's full of life

with many treasures

Take what you want

Just leave me with a simple memory

Of you and your shining orbs

Of your honest smile

Despite your grumbling demeanor, Loneliness
just doesn't suit you

To Be In Love

I'm not really a broken woman

I have my moments

I try not to dwell on my insecurities,

On my bad days, I'm a crybaby and sometimes it
is hard to accept criticism as

I'm such a prideful person

I've come to terms with the fact I don't have a
single ounce of talent in my body

much less athleticism

If the world ended today, I probably wouldn't
survive to be quite frank

I have a hot temper but my wrath is weak

When my scathing heart catches sight of you

When you give me that tender smile

In rare cases I'm a comedian lighting up the
room

In many others, I'm clearing a room with my
gloom and doom

I'm not meant to live in the spotlight yet I can't
see myself living an 8-5

You turn me into a love-sick teenager

I'm noticing everything about you

From your funny mannerisms to the pet peeves
that bother you
I stumbled onto your love language and I never
saw a man's eyes sparkle in

delight

I'm in my waste of daydreams now

And I never burned so bright

To Be In Love

My tiny wings always flutter at the sight of you

Stars in my eyes catch you by surprise

In a room full of pretty men, I can only stare at
you

You don't know what to do but relish in my
attention I give you

We find ourselves stuck together forever, a
contract signed in blood

When tragedy strikes, we are broken
Just stay with me in this chaos, it'll only be for a
moment

Just so we can soak in the pain

This sorrow, this angst, this lack of luck

This is what it feels like to be mortal

To be in love

Through these tough times, I love how your
heavy hand tightens around my

fingers

The clenching of your teeth loosening when I
caress your face

Weariness in your wrinkles dissipates

I'll help you regain that sense of control when
you can't find it in the world

To be that consistent ever-changing yet so
predictable variable in your life.

When the world beats you down, cry in my arms
even if it's just for tonight,

wake up a man so fierce and powerful

enemies will tremble

build the empire as Marcus Aurelius would have

that stands tall to the heavens

so ethereal and bright

I'll Remember You

Put on my oversized sweater dear

No need to catch your death

Nights like this are unkind to a lone stranger

Big brother's watchers in the windows whisper

I'm uneasy about letting you leave, I fear the
feeling in my bones

Yet you managed to console my cries

With a warm embrace and a few cheesy words.

"They'll have to kill me before they can keep me
away from you"

I can't help but smile and snort softly

A moment of distraction with puerility and
laughter

We say our bittersweet goodbyes and end with a
chaste kiss on delicate lips

As you walk out the door, I wonder if I'll ever
see you again

I wait, wait, and wait to hear your voice

I fidget and bite at my nails until they bleed and
throb

A habit I thought I killed off long ago

I can't stay seated in the chair near my window
and my mind races, so troubled I

am

Worst scenarios plague my mind of you

In ditches off somewhere, I can't reach you

Get caught by flashes of light past curfew

Get caught in the mind of a freeborn man

and I'll never get to hold your hand again.

My rock in these daunting times.

My sunshine on gloomy days.

They'll take you away, regardless of your
notoriety and character

They falsely accuse you of what they see fit and
you'll cease to exist

No one will remember you. I'll lose all of you

2. 3. 4. Days

No word from you

What should I do?

I'm so furious with you as well as myself for not
convincing you to stay

Now, They'll take me away and erase you from
my feeble mind

I can't help but fall to my knees and wail loudly

I rock back and forth clutching my arms so
tightly
Hours it's been, I've quieted.

Just staring and picking at the floorboards 'til I
dozed off curled up in my own arms

Bang Bang Bang! They have finally come for
me.

trembling, I wished you would take my hand and
run off into the night.

I miss you so much.

They locked me up for good

They said I deserved solitary confinement

for my association with you

I was a traitor in their eyes, a terrible sinner

I never cared and I still don't, I hope you know
that.

On pieces of toilet paper and some lead, I
swiped from the guard

I scribbled down all my memories of you.

Of all the trouble we got into

Of all the jokes you used to tell

Of all the dreams we shared

I'll remember exactly how you used to tease me

When I flushed at your advances

I'll remember the odd way you would cradle
your mugs

I'll remember every line every contour of your
handsome face

The way your eyes crinkled when you laughed

at the look on my face when I burnt dinner on
accident

or whenever I blurt out something silly

The way you would hold me at night after a
harsh day

You are the only thing keeping me sane whilst
I'm at my lowest

They try to break me down 'til I'm an empty
shell, but

with these paper memories tucked away inside
the crumbling concrete walls,

I can find my way back to you

They'll have to kill me before I'll forget you.

Wise and Cultured

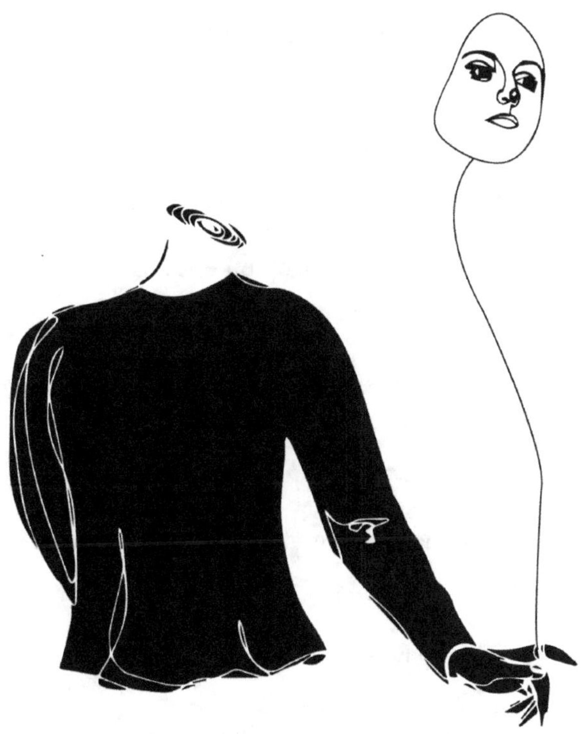

I push down my dark delight

Seeing others despair over my words

I can be so cruel and conceited

I should take a double-take

Before I won't be able to find my way back

Everyone wants to rule the world

Everyone wants to be special

Everyone wants to believe they are righteous

I'm no better than the people I criticize

I want to have a legacy in this world

I want to be special even if it's to one person

I want to believe I'm in the right but I could be
wrong

I know this to be true

It's in the back of my mind like angry bees in a
hive

I will always ponder

What it will be like to be wise and cultured.

I fear God is real

I fear that God is real

I fear I live under the scrutiny and whims of the devil

My life is a gamble, Every decision and every move I make

will cause my rows of dominoes to fall, good or bad. If I choose wrong,

I could fall into ruin.

If I choose right, paradise would be in my sights

I'm at stalemate, wearily turning to each door in
uncertainty

of where they would lead me

What does it mean to truly have sunk into
christianity?

To have let go of my vices and of other ways I
have tarnished myself?
My desperate control relinquished?

How do I find comfort in the scriptures

When my understanding of its poetry is lacking?

When its interpretations vary

I'm blind to what others see

I'm teetering on the edge of beauty and darkness

Yet I can't will myself to just believe

Dear, Stranger

Dear stranger,

I haven't met you but I'm here

Don't give up on me yet

I'm trying to be better

To become what no one else is

To provide something that no one else can for you

To be irreplaceable, no need to stray

I want to be the one that you share memories with

I want to be able to speak to you with just my eyes

Read you like the back of my hand

To know every mole, every scar

What your silence means or every expression you make

The actions you would likely take

Your funny mannerisms, your terrible humor, the little things you do

These moments I will take to heaven if I can't have you by my side where I take

that last breath. Cherish hushed conversations
that last until the sun wakes.

where the earth meets the sky. We can dream
about the past, present, and

future. I need you to tell me your thoughts, your
desires, your dreams.

What are your needs and where do your
boundaries lie?

Where can I push you to your limit? I know this
vulnerability takes time.

I can take my time, I can wait years until you are
ready to speak

To have such deeply seated trust, I know how
you will break

Shared trauma I will take to the grave with you
and only you.

This vow I make to share these intimate
moments with you

This oath is to stay for eternity, hell is to pay if broken

Birdcage

I'm in the birdcage of my own making. I've
trapped myself and I can't bear to see

the sun. It might be the self-hatred that I've
caught from the parasites in the

depths of my own mind. They've been waiting a
long time. They don't tell me to

die. It's quite the opposite. If I die, they do too.

I'll feel the suffering when it's my turn. It's only
a matter of time. It'll happen

when I step out of the cage. From the safety of
comfort, I've been building,

protecting, and attempting to preserve amongst a
world crumbling around me.

I don't know what I'll do when I crumble too.

I know you won't be there. You are but a dream.
So far away. You don't even
know my name. Like Lana would say, you are
my living legend.

Glimpse of Eden

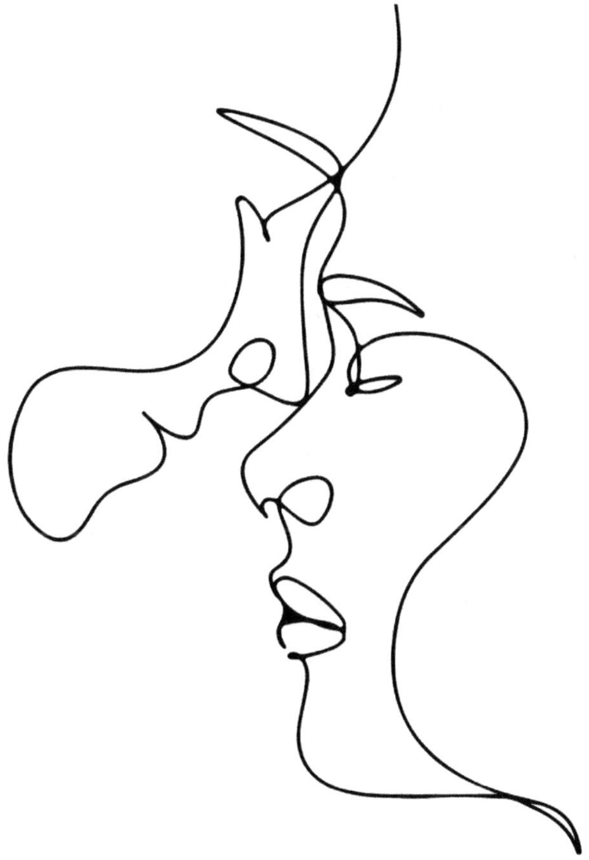

Beauty in the softness of her curves and his
vigor strong as steel

germaniums as red as her cheeks flushed a rosy
hue and hydrangeas cool as

her man's melancholy blues.

He blooms in chaotic doom, seduces her to sing

along in her own familiar tune

Don't leave her lonely and weary

The night doesn't have to be dreary

From the moment he asked for her hand,

He knew the stars in her eyes must never die

Pretty girl with a clever tongue,

he can't help but smile remembering the times of
playful banter

She is the apple of heaven's eyes

Despite her mortality and lack of grace

He won her affection with humility and charm

He danced her around Roman pillars of an
ancient gazebo of stone, picked her a

flower the shade of her cherry lips

God's playground has plenty of room, maybe for
a bundle of joy or two

Lay upon white marble, caress her snowy
silhouette

Hear the gentle weeping of a waterfall as a tree
nymph sings a lullaby

Forget the day that will come to pass

That this is a fleeing dream

This forbidden desire for

Her Glimpse of Eden

Wasteland daydreams

I left my body in the rain

In the passenger seat of an old beat-up truck

Whites of my eyes for all to see

I'm not dead at least not yet

I'm dreaming, wasting away

I live to die, die to live

Deep breathes are a struggle

Inhale a bit of my hallucinations

Of the hands squeezing me tight

Of him painting my lips the deepest shade of red

Of him staring into the windows of my eyes

If I don't move away, he'll know exactly what
goes on inside
He'll know of the storms brewing that he has
been oblivious to

I don't want to move, I'm desperate for him to
know what I'm thinking and dreaming of.

My words have no meaning, as I am speechless

Of the moonlight that glides over his face

Of the liquid tenderness in his eyes

My wasteland is nothing but him.

Where the tree limbs have lost their leaves

Cold desert sands linger as long as he remains
unaware

Where nature lost her glowing hues

This dilapidated old house is safe

To haunt these dead spaces

In the middle of nowhere
I can remain here wrapped in a worn blanket.

Only then did Fear rear from its slumber, rattling
my mind, trampling over what

little I have

I whisper, pull me in a warm embrace, Run your
fingers through my hair, and

Read to me until I wake.

Don't let the reaper come in through my feeble
doors, to come for what's yours to take.

I'm not ready to let you go just yet.
And so he did until everything fell silent

Hide and Seek

It's almost midnight

A humid summer night

Creaky windows open

I can't escape the heat or my troubled mind

Not even in tank tops and boy shorts

Sleep is not coming home tonight

Lovecraft tales to stave off the boredom

Feeling something missing, I glance at my
telephone

Should I?

I lost my nerve. I was going to let you be yet

You caught me by surprise

You call me up at 3 am
As if I sent my thoughts to you

I answer wide-eyed

You wanna play hide and seek tonight?

Temptation beckons me

I do want to play

To run around in the night

dancing around in city lights

Share an icy treat on a park bench my head on
your shoulder

Dash your nose in whipped cream, failing to
whip my tongue in cherry knots

Blindfolded, I spin you around

No peeking I cry

1,2,3 you count

I Run, run, run. Hide. hide. Hide
Until you catch me

Like a bad man in the night

Hiding in bushes when you call for me

Less than a foot away from me

You stood, puzzled heavy breathes

I stare you down

prey in my sights

I catch you by surprise

Laughter never seemed so beautiful

Like children we are

We play, play, and play in the darkness

We can forget the insomnia plaguing our minds

Concrete rooftops, starry night

Soul river streams collide

You electrify, you breathe through me

We live on the same wavelengths

Whispering all our secret fancies

Hear my heart scream in delight

Dawn rises

oranges and violets

Kisses so sweet

Cotton candy dreams

Voice of a lullaby

I'll lie next to you in the early morning

resting In your arms, darling I know I'll be
alright

Dark Angel

50

He sings sweet things

With battered broken wings

Bareback scarred

He's fierce and lonely

So I painted his red roses black

To show he was my one and only

Another Life

In my dream,

He sings softly, his hands ghosting over the
piano in a restful harmony,

he makes the sounds of sadness and regret so
lovely, that he cries for salvation

A voice in my mind compels me to ponder about
him

Enamored, I write to his forlorn mourning with a
heavy heart

Knowing full well I will get no reply

Much like Orpheus, he could bring Hades to
tears

and make the whole world weep with his gentle
rumbling

I begin to dance with the unseen. An invisible
hand guided me around the
ballroom.

He appeared to me, the piano continuing to play
on its own

Taking the lead, he puts my arms around his
neck, twirls me around in the night

I don't want to continue this dance with anyone
but him

Even if this sweet image of him will fade as my
youth will wane

Even as I grow feeble and decrepit

till death whispers my name as my lips turn a
shade of icy blue

I'll let him draw upon my strings like a breath of
wind,

make my delicate body move to resonate a
melancholy tune.

I'm frozen in time forever locked in repetition,
in a single motion

I wished I could remain here looking at the stars
in his eyes

He'd like to keep me like this forever dancing at
his whims

Yet, my life was fated to remain short and

this obsession with vengeance, the degradation
of his ancient mind

Will continue to bring about disaster and death

With his fury, this village will remain abandoned

History shed in blood and strife

If I can bring him peace of mind, there's hope
for him.   55

Hope for us in another life.

Candelabra

Light the candelabra

I wanna see your silhouette in the soft light of
the flames just this once

Shadows envelop your features in the most
sensual way

Before you leave me in this garden of our hell

Let me burn this blurry image of you into my
memory

I'll locate your love while you pluck the strings
of your heart

I hear your somber lullabies, I can listen, play
along

I give up my eyes, I need to show I have no need
for my sight

These droplets of blood from my sockets are a
minor inconvenience

Pay no mind to the aches inside

In the void of my desires and my convictions to
show the world I'm capable of

giving and receiving affection

I'm lonely, I only wish to find my way to you
again before

the minotaur swallows me whole

Blind, I feel my way through the labyrinth of
these corridors

Hand of night guides me to you

encompass me in your own darkness,

keep me hidden from the monster lurking in my
own

drain the poison from the vein

Take my hand, accompany me back into the
light

We are lost no more

Disciple or Lover

Opulence and pearls

Dainty dresses and perfume of sweet flowers

I lay upon my window in the tallest towers

Thinking how I would forgo the comfort, spend
my days, starting over, repenting

of my obvious spoils to remain in the presence
of you.

How could I be best helpful to you?

You have given me many reasons to believe you
are worthy of my complete

submission

Your dreams are mine as mine are yours

As I write for hours in the candlelight, I wrestle
with these words you lent me.

It brings me such delight.

My heart flutters when we bicker with
heavy-lidded eyes.

Disciple or lover.

I would follow you to the ends of the earth to see
your spirit burn bright

Teapot

These tumultuous waters have fractured my delicate teapot

Broken teacups can never hold liquid shards of
my heart

He was foreseen in the leaves as the one who
could refill my cup

He could repair the remnants of my very being

If I could just see clearly through clouded eyes

I would have known he had a teapot of cast iron

Courageous and defiant

He stands the tests of time

And he's all mine

Ocean Eyes

Seafoam green specks of deep blue

Heavy soft billows gravitate

Into the deep void of his pupils

Dear God

Dear God,

Have mercy on us as we confront our demons

That the foreboding forces do not have dominion
over our minds

Wipe away the decay in the temple of our bosom

Purify our blood with the clearest of waters

That by the end of the day, we will be holy once
again

That the people at my side are given amnesty as

They make their way back to you.

I beg you to guide them as they remain lost,

the tunnel of light remains unseen by the hazy
fog

That drowns us in strife and confusion

Amen.